DOING MARRIAGE GOD'S WAY

THE PRACTICES

GROUP PARTICIPANT GUIDE

JIMMY EVANS

DOING MARRIAGE GOD'S WAY

THE PRACTICES

GROUP PARTICIPANT GUIDE

JIMMY EVANS

XO
PUBLISHING

XO
PUBLISHING

Doing Marriage God's Way: The Practices: Group Participant Guide
Copyright © 2025 by Jimmy Evans

ISBN: 978-1-960870-68-1 eBook
ISBN: 978-1-960870-71-1 Paperback

XO Publishing is a leading creator of relationship-based resources. We focus primarily on marriage-related content for churches, small group curriculum, and people looking for timeless truths about relationships and overall marital health. For more information on other resources from XO Publishing, visit XOPublishing.com.

XO Publishing
1021 Grace Lane
Southlake, TX 76092

While the authors make every effort to provide accurate URLs at the time of printing for external or third-party internet websites, neither they nor the publisher assume any responsibility for changes or errors made after publication.

Printed in the United States of America

25 26 27 28—5 4 3 2 1

Table of Contents

Introduction

Welcome!

Welcome to *Doing Marriage God's Way: The Practices!* If you've completed the Foundations course, you understand the biblical laws that make marriage work. Now it's time to put those principles into daily practice. This manual is your personal workbook for reflection, activities, and application during your group sessions.

HOW TO USE THIS MANUAL:

- Bring this manual to every session.
- Complete reflection exercises during your personal time.
- Use the spaces provided for notes during video teaching.
- Be honest in your assessments—growth requires honesty.
- Apply the homework consistently for best results.

GROUP GUIDELINES:

- What's shared here, stays here (practice confidentiality).
- Speak for yourself, not your spouse.
- Listen to understand, not to give advice.
- Honor different perspectives and marriage seasons.
- Focus on growth, not perfection.

SESSION 1

How to Understand and
Meet Your Wife's Needs

KEY SCRIPTURE

"Husbands, love your wives, just as Christ also loved the church and gave Himself for her..."

—Ephesians 5:25

VIDEO TEACHING NOTES

- The four basic needs that women have are: _____, _____, _____, and _____.

- **Security** means that you are _____ serving her and _____ care of her.

- **Non-sexual affection** means that you're _____ with her without just touching her in _____ ways.

- **Open and honest communication** means including her _____ and letting your wife ask you _____.

- **Leadership** means that they want you to be the loving _____ of the wellbeing of children, the _____, _____, romance.

- Nothing makes a wife feel more secure than a _____, _____ man.

- Nothing makes a wife feel more insecure than a _____, _____ man.

- The question "Are you _____?" means: If there's anything I'm not doing, or if there's a need in you that I'm not meeting, I will do whatever it takes to make sure it's taken care of.

- Marriage only works when you _____ at it.

PERSONAL REFLECTION: WIFE'S NEEDS ASSESSMENT

For Wives—Rate how well these needs are currently being met (1–10):

Security (Feeling sacrificially served and put first): ____ /10

- I feel like I come first in my husband's priorities.
- He asks, "Are you okay?" and really listens.
- He serves me with a willing heart.
- I feel safe and cared for.

Non-Sexual Affection (Tender touch without agenda): ____ /10

- He holds my hand regularly.
- He hugs me without it leading to sex.
- He is physically tender and gentle with me.
- I feel valued beyond just being a sexual partner.

Open and Honest Communication (Detailed conversations): ____ /10

- We have daily face-to-face conversation time.
- He shares details about his day and feelings.
- He patiently answers my questions.
- I feel emotionally connected to him.

Leadership (Loving initiative in home/finances/spirituality): ____ /10

- He takes initiative in spiritual matters.
- He leads in financial planning and decisions.
- He is involved in parenting decisions.
- I feel like we're a team with him leading in a loving way.

For Husbands—Self Assessment:

Which of your wife's needs do you struggle most to understand or meet?

_____

What would change if you truly adopted the mindset "I'm not okay until you're okay"?

_____

REFLECTION QUESTIONS

For Wives:

Which need feels most important to you right now, and why?

_____

For Husbands:

How does it feel to hear that your wife has different needs than you do?

_____

For Both:

How can understanding these specific needs change the way you serve each other?

_____

THIS WEEK'S APPLICATION

Husbands:

☐ Ask your wife "Are you okay?" every day this week and really listen.

Wives:

☐ Clearly communicate one specific need to your husband.

Both:

☐ Protect one hour daily for face-to-face conversation with no distractions.

NOTES

SESSION 2

How to Understand and Meet Your Husband's Needs

KEY SCRIPTURE

"Nevertheless let each one of you in particular so love his own wife as himself, and let the wife see that she respects her husband."

—Ephesians 5:33

VIDEO TEACHING NOTES

- The four core needs that men have are: _____, _____, _____, and _____.
- **Honor** is the _____ need of men.
- We need _____ and we're very sensitive in our _____.
- The more you _____ your husband, the more you're going to get to his heart.
- **Sex**—most sex in marriage is not because one person is in the mood, it's because the _____ person's in the mood.
- The secret of sexual fulfillment in marriage is a _____ spirit.
- **Friendship**—we want to be _____ with our wives.
- **Domestic support** means that you're domestically _____.
- Women have the gift of _____ that men don't have.
- Sometimes you just have to let your husband _____.
- The _____ principle says if you fill that vessel with honor, the cork is going to rise.
- When you're fighting fire with fire, you get a bigger fire. But when you fight fire with _____, it changed our marriage.

7

PERSONAL REFLECTION: HUSBAND'S NEEDS ASSESSMENT

For Husbands—Rate how well these needs are currently being met (1-10):

Honor (Respect, appreciation, being treated well): _____/10

- My wife speaks to me respectfully.
- She appreciates what I do for the family.
- She treats me like I'm valuable and important.
- She doesn't criticize or control me.

Sex (Physical intimacy and sexual fulfillment): _____/10

- We have regular physical intimacy.
- My wife is willing and available sexually.
- I feel desired by my wife.
- Sex is not a source of conflict between us.

Friendship (Being buddies, doing things together): _____/10

- My wife enjoys spending time with me.
- She participates in activities I enjoy.
- I feel like she's my best friend.
- We have fun together.

Domestic Support (Home being peaceful and welcoming): _____/10

- Our home feels like a sanctuary.
- My wife takes pride in our home environment.
- She creates a peaceful atmosphere.
- I feel welcome and comfortable at home.

For Wives—Self Assessment:

Which of your husband's needs do you struggle most to understand or meet?

_____

How do you typically respond when your husband fails or disappoints you?

_____

THE HONOR CHALLENGE

For Wives:

Think of a recent situation where your husband failed or made a mistake. How could you have applied the "cork principle"—filling the vessel with honor instead of trying to fix the problem with criticism?

_____

_____

_____

_____

_____

_____

_____

_____

REFLECTION QUESTIONS

For Husbands:

When do you feel most honored and respected vs. most criticized or controlled?

_____

For Wives:

How difficult is it to honor your husband when he doesn't seem to deserve it?

_____

For Both:

How might prayer be more effective than confrontation in changing each other?

_____

THIS WEEK'S APPLICATION

Wives:

- ☐ Practice the cork principle—honor your husband even when he doesn't deserve it.

Husbands:

- ☐ Respond positively to honor and work to become worthy of respect.

Both:

- ☐ Wives pray for husbands daily instead of criticizing.

NOTES

SESSION 3

Communication: Building Your Bridge

KEY SCRIPTURE

"Instead, speaking the truth in love, we will grow to become in every respect the mature body of him who is the head, that is, Christ."

—Ephesians 4:15

VIDEO TEACHING NOTES

- Speaking the _____ in love—we grow. Truth and _____ have to go together.
- The five keys to communication in marriage:
  1. _____—you can't communicate with a person who doesn't care.
  2. _____—listening means my heart is engaged.
  3. _____—we enter into God's gates with thanksgiving and into his courts with praise.
  4. _____—speaking the truth in love.
  5. _____—the opposite of openness is defensiveness.
- The difference between _____ and _____:
- **Criticizing:** "You always do this because you're _____ like your mother..."
- **Complaining:** "When you said that to me yesterday, I have no idea what you meant. Can I tell you how it made me _____?"
- When you're starting a confrontation, begin by saying "_____."
- We need to sit down face to face for at least _____ a day.

13

COMMUNICATION ASSESSMENT

Rate your current communication skills (1-10):

Caring (Making your spouse feel heard and valued):

- I make eye contact when my spouse is talking: _____/10
- I eliminate distractions during important conversations: _____/10
- My spouse knows I care about what they're saying: _____/10

Listening (Hearing heart, not just words):

- I listen to understand, not just to respond: _____/10
- I ask follow-up questions to understand better: _____/10
- My spouse feels truly heard by me: _____/10

Praising (Speaking life, not death):

- I regularly praise and encourage my spouse: _____/10
- I focus on positives more than negatives: _____/10
- My words build up rather than tear down: _____/10

Confronting (Complaining vs. criticizing):

- I address issues without attacking character: _____/10
- I use "I feel" statements rather than "you always": _____/10
- I start difficult conversations with love and commitment: _____/10

Openness (Non-defensive responses):

- I listen without defending when my spouse has concerns: _____/10
- I'm willing to hear feedback about my behavior: _____/10
- I work toward solutions rather than winning arguments: _____/10

PRACTICE EXERCISE: COMPLAINT VS. CRITICISM

Think of something your spouse does that bothers you. Write it both ways:

- **Criticism format (don't do this):** "You always _____ because you're _____."

- **Complaint format (do this):** "When _____ happened, I felt _____. Can we talk about it?"

DAILY COMMUNICATION COMMITMENT

Our daily face-to-face time will be:

Time: _____ Location: _____ No phones: ☐ No TV: ☐
No distractions: ☐

REFLECTION QUESTIONS

1. Which of the five communication keys is strongest in your marriage? Which needs the most work?

   _____

2. How has criticism damaged your communication? How could complaining help instead?

   _____

3. What would change if you had one hour of distraction-free conversation daily?

   _____

THIS WEEK'S APPLICATION

- ☐ Practice the five keys to communication daily.
- ☐ Have at least one hour of face-to-face conversation each day.
- ☐ Practice complaining (expressing needs) instead of criticizing (attacking character).
- ☐ Give three specific praises to your spouse daily.

NOTES

_____

_____

_____

_____

_____

_____

_____

_____

_____

_____

_____

_____

_____

_____

_____

_____

_____

_____

SESSION 4

Money: Seven Principles for Financial Success

KEY SCRIPTURE

"Bring all the tithes into the storehouse, that there may be food in My house, and try Me now in this," says the Lord of hosts, "If I will not open for you the windows of heaven and pour out for you such blessing that there will not be room enough to receive it."

—Malachi 3:10

VIDEO TEACHING NOTES

- There are _____ different ways that people see money (money languages).

  1. **Driver**—they see money as _____.
  2. **Analytic**—they see money as _____.
  3. **Amiable**—they see money as _____.
  4. **Expressive**—they see money as _____.

- The number one principle is _____—I need to respect my spouse's different perspective on money.

- **Partnership**—make all your financial decisions _____.

- **Stewardship**—the first thing we do when we get paid is we _____ to the Lord.

- **Contentment**—godliness with contentment is a means of great _____.

- When you're doing things God's way, you're rowing with the _____.

- Debt _____ the joy of whatever you own.

18

MONEY LANGUAGE ASSESSMENT

Circle the money language that most fits you:

Driver (Money = Success)

- I see money as a way to achieve and accomplish.
- I like to make financial decisions quickly.
- I'm motivated by financial goals and winning.
- I measure success by financial achievement.

Analytic (Money = Security)

- I see money as protection against uncertainty.
- I prefer to save and be conservative with money.
- I want to avoid financial risk.
- I feel secure when I have money saved.

Amiable (Money = Love)

- I see money as a way to express care and love.
- I enjoy giving gifts and creating experiences.
- I like to use money to bless others.
- Generosity makes me feel good.

Expressive (Money = Acceptance)

- I see money as a way to fit in and be accepted.
- I enjoy nice things and experiences.
- I like money for what it can do socially.
- I want to look successful to others.

FINANCIAL HEALTH CHECK

Rate your current financial situation (1–10):

- Respect for different money perspectives: _____/10
- Partnership in financial decisions: _____/10
- Regular giving/tithing: _____/10
- Living below your means: _____/10
- Freedom from debt stress: _____/10

COUPLE'S MONEY LANGUAGES

My money language: _____. My spouse's money language: _____.

How are they different? _____.

How have you judged your spouse's approach to money? _____.

How could your different approaches actually help you make better decisions?

_____

REFLECTION QUESTIONS

1. How has misunderstanding your spouse's money language caused conflict in your marriage?

   _____

2. What would change if you started giving/tithing as your first financial priority?

   _____

3. How does debt or financial pressure affect your relationship?

   _____

THIS WEEK'S APPLICATION

- ☐ Apologize for any judgment about your spouse's money language.
- ☐ Decide together on a spending limit that requires mutual agreement.
- ☐ Start or increase your giving to your local church.
- ☐ Schedule a monthly budget meeting to make financial decisions together.

NOTES

_____

_____

_____

_____

_____

_____

_____

_____

_____

_____

_____

_____

_____

_____

_____

_____

_____

_____

SESSION 5

Practicing Safe Technology

KEY SCRIPTURE

"Therefore a man shall leave his father and mother and be joined to his wife, and they shall become one flesh."

—Genesis 2:24

VIDEO TEACHING NOTES

Key statistics about technology and marriage:

- _____% of divorces start as online affairs.
- _____% of divorce attorneys report increased use of social media evidence.
- 1 in _____ married people contemplate divorce due to their spouse's social media activity.
- _____% of Americans admit phone addiction.
- Americans check their phone _____ times a day.
- _____% of people admit to checking phones during sex.

The real problem:

We can't be _____ anymore.

Three rules of intimacy:

1. Intimacy requires _____.
2. Intimacy requires _____ human contact.
3. Intimacy requires _____ and boundaries.

- Technology is a wonderful _____ but a terrible _____.

- If you can't turn your phone off, you don't _____ it— it _____ you.

- When you're on your phone, you have to _____ it and _____ at it—taking your two most important areas for intimacy.

TECHNOLOGY REALITY CHECK

Check your phone settings for this week's screen time:

- Hours per day on phone: _____
- Most used apps: _____
- Times checked per day: _____

Rate these statements (1–10, 10 being "always true"):

- I can have a conversation without checking my phone: ____/10
- My spouse gets my full attention when they're talking: ____/10
- We have phone-free time together daily: ____/10
- Technology never comes between us during intimate moments: ____/10
- I can turn off my phone without anxiety: ____/10

Current Technology Habits

Check all that apply to you:

- ☐ I answer my phone during conversations with my spouse.
- ☐ I check my phone while my spouse is talking to me.
- ☐ I use devices in the bedroom.
- ☐ I have passwords that my spouse doesn't know.
- ☐ I check social media more than 5 times per day.
- ☐ I feel anxious when I can't check my phone.
- ☐ Technology sometimes comes before my spouse's needs.

TECHNOLOGY BOUNDARIES NEEDED

Device-Free Times I Need:

- Daily: From _____ to _____ (minimum 1 hour)
- During meals: Yes / No
- In bedroom: Yes / No
- During important conversations: Yes / No

Device-Free Zones I Need:

- ☐ Bedroom
- ☐ Dining room
- ☐ Car
- ☐ Date nights
- ☐ Other _____

REFLECTION QUESTIONS

1. How has technology hurt your ability to be intimate and present with your spouse?

   _____

2. What boundaries do you most need to establish to protect your marriage?

   _____

3. How would your relationship change if you prioritized face-to-face time over digital connection?

   _____

THIS WEEK'S APPLICATION

- ☐ Establish clear device-free times and zones.
- ☐ Share all passwords with your spouse for complete transparency.
- ☐ Complete a technology fast (choose: one evening device-free, no phones during meals, no devices in bedroom, or one day without social media).
- ☐ Prioritize one hour of daily phone-free time together.

NOTES

SESSION 6

When You're Building Alone and Moving Forward

KEY SCRIPTURE

"Wives, in the same way submit yourselves to your own husbands so that, if any of them do not believe the word, they may be won over without words by the behavior of their wives, when they see the purity and reverence of your lives."

—1 Peter 3:1–2

VIDEO TEACHING NOTES

- Sometimes one spouse wants a good marriage and another spouse _____.
- This is called _____ love—doing the right thing when your spouse is doing the wrong thing.

Important distinction:

- **Suffering:** being _____, going through difficulty.
- **Abuse:** _____, harm, violence—you should not put up with this.

Four principles when you're building alone:

1. _____ to God—"I want my marriage, but I'll do it God's way."
2. Willingness to _____—going through difficulty righteously (not abuse)
3. _____—believing God for the marriage He wants you to have
4. _____ support—having mature, godly people pray with you
   - When Karen was fighting fire with fire, she got a bigger _____.
   - When she fought fire with _____, it changed our marriage.
   - Your spouse can be _____ without words as they observe your pure, respectful behavior.

PERSONAL ASSESSMENT

If both spouses are equally committed:

Use this session to understand how to help others and practice redemptive love in smaller conflicts.

If one spouse is less committed:

Answer honestly without defensiveness.

Current Situation Assessment:

- Are both of you equally committed to making your marriage work? ☐ Yes ☐ No

  If no, who is carrying more of the load? _____
- Are there areas where one spouse is destructive or unwilling to change? ☐ Yes ☐ No
- **Is there abuse present?** (Physical, verbal, emotional harm) ☐ Yes—Seek help immediately ☐ No

THE FOUR PRINCIPLES IN PRACTICE

1. **Submission to God**—Instead of using threats, manipulation, or revenge, I will:

   _____

2. **Willingness to Suffer (not abuse)**—I accept that change takes time, and I will:

   _____

3. **Vision**—I will pray Ephesians 5 over my spouse and believe God for:

   _____

5. **Positive Support**—Mature, godly people who will pray with me:

   ◆ _____

   ◆ _____

REDEMPTIVE LOVE IN ACTION

This week, I will practice redemptive love by:

1. Treating my spouse better than they deserve
2. Doing the right thing when they do the wrong thing
3. Praying instead of nagging or criticizing
4. Serving instead of demanding

Specific actions I will take:

_____

_____

_____

_____

_____

_____

_____

_____

_____

_____

_____

_____

_____

_____

_____

_____

REFLECTION QUESTIONS

1. How could redemptive love change your specific marriage situation?

   _____

2. Which of the four principles is hardest for you to practice? Why?

   _____

3. What would it look like to trust God completely with your spouse's heart while you focus on doing the right thing?

   _____

THIS WEEK'S APPLICATION

- ☐ Practice redemptive love regardless of your spouse's response.
- ☐ Pray for your spouse daily instead of trying to change them with words.
- ☐ Get support from mature, godly friends who will pray with you.
- ☐ Read and pray Ephesians 5 over your marriage daily.

NOTES

Course Review

Putting It All Together

THE SIX PRACTICES SUMMARY

1. **Understanding Wife's Needs:** Security, Non-sexual Affection, Communication, Leadership
2. **Understanding Husband's Needs:** Honor, Sex, Friendship, Domestic Support
3. **Communication:** Caring, Listening, Praising, Confronting (complaining not criticizing), Openness
4. **Financial Success:** Respect money languages, Partnership in decisions, Giving first, Contentment
5. **Safe Technology:** Privacy, Human contact, Boundaries—Technology as servant not master
6. **Building Alone/Redemptive Love:** Submission to God, Willingness to suffer, Vision, Positive support

BIGGEST TAKEAWAYS

What are the three most important things you've learned in this course?

1. _____
2. _____
3. _____

30-DAY ACTION PLAN

Choose your top priority from the course and create a specific plan:

My Priority:

(Circle one)

- Meeting Spouse's Needs
- Communication Skills
- Financial Partnership
- Technology Boundaries
- Redemptive Love

Why this is my priority:

_____

Daily Action:

I will _____ .

Weekly Action:

I will _____ .

Accountability:

I will check in with _____ .

Marriage Practices Vision

Complete this statement with your spouse:

"With God's help, we commit to practicing these biblical principles daily. We will serve each other's needs, communicate with truth and love, partner in our finances, keep technology in its proper place, and practice redemptive love. Our marriage will be marked by..."

_____

_____

_____

_____

_____

_____

_____

_____

_____

_____

Signatures:

Husband: _____ Date: _____

Wife: _____ Date: _____

Final Encouragement

You don't have to practice these perfectly—just consistently. Use these biblical practices daily. When you fail, practice redemptive love. When you succeed, stay humble. Remember that marriage is built through daily choices, not just understanding principles.

> "Unless the Lord builds the house,
> they labor in vain who build it."

> —Psalm 127:1

Let God build your house through these daily practices.

Quick Reference

WIFE'S FOUR NEEDS:

1. **Security**—Sacrificial service, being put first
2. **Non-sexual Affection**—Tender touch without agenda
3. **Open Communication**—Detailed conversations, emotional connection
4. **Leadership**—Loving initiative in home, finances, spirituality

HUSBAND'S FOUR NEEDS:

1. **Honor**—Respect, appreciation, being treated well
2. **Sex**—Physical intimacy and sexual fulfillment
3. **Friendship**—Being buddies, doing activities together
4. **Domestic Support**—Home being peaceful and welcoming

COMMUNICATION KEYS:

1. **Caring**—Eye contact, undistracted attention
2. **Listening**—Hearing heart, not just words
3. **Praising**—Speaking life, encouragement
4. **Confronting**—Complaining (expressing needs) not criticizing (attacking character)
5. **Openness**—Non-defensive responses

MONEY LANGUAGES:

1. **Driver** = Success
2. **Analytic** = Security
3. **Amiable** = Love
4. **Expressive** = Acceptance

TECHNOLOGY RULES:

- Intimacy requires privacy, human contact, boundaries.
- Technology is servant, not master.
- Daily device-free time is essential.

BUILDING ALONE:

1. Submit to God
2. Willingness to suffer (not abuse)
3. Vision for God's best
4. Positive support

EMERGENCY PHRASES:

- "Are you okay?"
- "I'm here to serve you."
- "I love you and I'm committed to our marriage."
- "How can I meet your needs better?"

www.ingramcontent.com/pod-product-compliance
Lightning Source LLC
Chambersburg PA
CBHW081644040426
42449CB00015B/3453